MW01042545

S19017

Walruses

*written and photographed
by Frank Staub*

Lerner Publications Company • Minneapolis, Minnesota

For Peggy, Mark, Tyler, and Ashton

Acknowledgments: Larry Van Daele, Kiana Koenen, and Steve Rice of the Alaska Department of Fish and Game; Don Winkleman and Kathy Yahr of Don's Round Island Boat Charters; Sarah Mesnick; and Joel Garlich-Miller of the U.S. Fish and Wildlife Service, who checked the manuscript for accuracy.

Additional photographs are reproduced with permission from: © Carleton Ray/Photo Researchers, Inc., pp. 10, 33, 34, 35, 36, 37, 38; © George Holton/Photo Researchers, Inc., p. 14; © Tom Walker/Visuals Unlimited, p. 19; © David B. Fleetham/Visuals Unlimited, p. 19; © Gerard Lacz/Animals Animals, p. 20; © Tom & Pat Leeson/Photo Researchers, Inc., p. 26; © Dan Guravich/Photo Researchers, Inc. , p. 31; © Steve Maslowski/Photo Researchers, Inc., p. 42.

Early Bird Nature Books were conceptualized by Ruth Berman and designed by Steve Foley. Series editor is Joelle Riley.

Text copyright © 1999 Lerner Publications Company
Photographs copyright © 1999 by Frank Staub unless otherwise noted

All rights reserved. International copyright secured. No part of this book may be reproduced, stored in a retrieval system, or transmitted in any form or by any means, electronic, mechanical, photocopying, recording, or otherwise, without the prior written permission of Lerner Publications Company, except for the inclusion of brief quotations in an acknowledged review.

Lerner Publications Company
A Division of the Lerner Publishing Group
241 First Avenue North
Minneapolis, MN 55401 U.S.A.

Website address: www.lernerbooks.com

Library of Congress Cataloging-in-Publication Data

Staub, Frank J.
    Walruses / written and photographed by Frank Staub.
        p.   cm. — (Early bird nature books)
    Includes index.
    Summary: Examines the physical characteristics, behavior, habitat, and life cycle of the walrus.
    ISBN 0–8225–3039–2 (alk. paper)
    1. Walruses—Juvenile literature. [1. Walruses.] I. Title.
    II. Series.
    QL737.P62S73   1999
    599.79'9—dc21   98-49072

Manufactured in the United States of America
1 2 3 4 5 6 – JR – 04 03 02 01 00 99

Contents

Map 5

Be a Word Detective 5

Chapter 1 **Big Teeth** 6

Chapter 2 **Living in Ice Water** . . 12

Chapter 3 **Swimming for Their Supper** 16

Chapter 4 **Living Together** 25

Chapter 5 **Growing Up** 33

Chapter 6 **People and Walruses** 40

On Sharing a Book 44
A NOTE TO ADULTS

Glossary 46

Index 47

Pacific walruses

Alaska (U.S.)

Atlantic walruses

CANADA

N

This map shows where walruses live in North America.

UNITED STATES

Be a Word Detective

Can you find these words as you read about the walrus's life? Be a detective and try to figure out what they mean. You can turn to the glossary on page 46 for help.

blubber   herds   prey
bull   ice floes   throat sacs
calf   nurses   tubercles
cow   pinnipeds   tusks
haul out   predators

5

Chapter 1

Walruses live to be about 40 years old. How big can a walrus grow?

Big Teeth

The walrus is one of the biggest animals on earth. Walruses can be more than 12 feet long. And they can weigh as much as 3,500 pounds. That's more than most cars weigh.

Walruses look a lot like their relatives, the seals and the sea lions. All these ocean animals are pinnipeds (PIN-nuh-pehdz). Instead of arms and legs, pinnipeds have four flippers. But walruses are the only pinnipeds with tusks. Tusks are teeth that never stop growing.

A walrus uses its flippers to help it move on land.

A walrus has two big tusks sticking out of its mouth. Both male and female walruses have tusks. Walrus tusks may grow up to 3 feet long. A walrus tusk can weigh up to 10 pounds. That's as much as a large sack of potatoes.

Sometimes walruses break their long tusks.

A walrus uses its flippers to swim in water.

Walrus tusks are made of ivory. Ivory is strong and hard. A walrus can dig its tusks into the ice to help pull itself out of the water. Walruses jab each other with their tusks. They also stab enemies with them. Sometimes walruses damage a tusk or break one off completely.

This walrus has dug its tusk into a block of ice. Sometimes walruses do this to take a rest when they are swimming.

Walruses have long front flippers. They use them mainly for steering when they swim.

Walruses use their back flippers to push their bodies forward in the water. On land, walruses turn their back flippers forward and downward. This helps hold up their bodies. Walruses walk on all four flippers.

Walruses spend about half their time in water and half on land.

Chapter 2

Sometimes walruses use their long tusks to scare or fight each other. How many kinds of walruses are there?

Living in Ice Water

There are two kinds of walruses. Atlantic walruses live in the Atlantic Ocean. Pacific walruses live in the Pacific Ocean. Pacific walruses are bigger than Atlantic walruses. Pacific walruses also have longer tusks than Atlantic walruses.

Both Atlantic and Pacific walruses live in the far north. The winters there are long and cold. But walruses don't get very cold. One reason is that they are so big. Heat stays in a big body longer than it stays in a small body.

The scientific name for walruses is Odobenus rosmarus.

These Atlantic walruses are near Moffen Island in the Arctic Ocean.

Walruses also stay warm because they have blubber. Blubber is a special layer of fat. It is just under the walrus's skin. A walrus's blubber can be 3 inches thick. Blubber holds in the walrus's body heat like a warm winter coat.

When a walrus gets cold, its skin turns white. That happens when a walrus stays in cold water for a long time. When a walrus gets hot, its skin turns pink or red. A hot walrus might lie on its back or hold a flipper in the air. This lets out some body heat. If the walrus is still too hot, it may go back into the icy water.

This walrus is lying on its back and waving a flipper in the air. It is trying to cool off.

Chapter 3

Walruses can swim underwater. How long can they stay underwater?

Swimming for Their Supper

Walruses are slow and clumsy on land. But they are good swimmers. Walruses can swim for hundreds of miles. They can dive 300 feet below the surface. And they can stay underwater for about 10 minutes.

When a walrus swims underwater it must hold its breath. That's because walruses are mammals. Mammals are animals who drink their mother's milk. Like people and other mammals, walruses must come to the water's surface to breathe air.

The water where walruses live is often covered with ice. A walrus must find holes in the ice to breathe through. A walrus can use its head and tusks to break breathing holes in the ice.

The light-colored walrus is cold. When it warms up, it will be the same color as the other walrus.

Walruses are predators (PREH-duh-turz). Predators are animals who hunt other animals for food. The animals predators hunt are called their prey. Walruses' prey are clams, worms, shrimps, snails, and other creatures who live on the ocean bottom. Walruses must swim to get to their food.

Walruses can swim long distances. But they are slow swimmers.

Polar bears and killer whales are predators who hunt walruses.

A walrus uses its whiskers to find food. To uncover its prey, the walrus digs with its lips. A walrus also squirts water from its mouth to move away the mud. If the walrus finds a clam, the walrus puts its lips around the shell. Then it sucks out the clam's body.

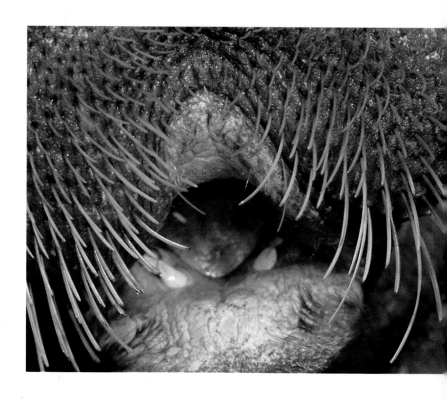

A walrus can't smell underwater. It uses its whiskers to find food.

Walruses eat a lot. A big walrus can eat 100 pounds of clams a day. To find the food it needs, a walrus may stay in the ocean for seven or eight days at a time. Between feeding trips, it rests on the shore or on the ice. A walrus rests for two or three days.

During long fishing trips, walruses can sleep while they float in the water. Walruses have special throat sacs that help them float. The throat sacs fill with air, like the inner tube you use at the beach. When a walrus sleeps in the water, it only has to lift its nose to breathe.

A female walrus is called a cow. Cows can blow up their lungs like balloons when they want to sleep at sea. The extra air in their lungs keeps them from sinking.

Walruses need a lot of rest between feeding trips.

This walrus's throat sac is filled with air.

Like other mammals, walruses must come to the surface of the water to breathe.

A male walrus is called a bull. A bull's throat sac helps him sing. Bulls sing underwater. Their songs sound like bells chiming far away. Singing is one way bulls talk.

Touching noses may help walruses get to know each other.

Walruses also make roaring or barking
sounds. Sometimes walruses talk by touching
noses. They look like they're kissing.

24

Chapter 4

These bulls are spending the summer on Round Island in Alaska. How many walruses are in a herd?

Living Together

Walruses live close together in groups called herds. A herd can have from 10 to more than 1,000 walruses. During most of the year, bulls and cows live in separate herds.

Sometimes walruses crowd together, even when there is no space left.

The place where walruses come ashore to rest is called a haul out. Walruses resting at a haul out lie close together. Sometimes they lie on top of each other.

Bulls have different ranks. A bull's rank is how important he is in the herd. Big bulls and bulls with long tusks usually have a higher rank than small bulls and bulls with short tusks.

A young bull is looking for a place to rest. All the other walruses are watching him.

As a bull moves through a herd, he looks at the other walruses' tusks. And they look at his. The bulls with the highest ranks get the best sleeping spots.

Bulls use their tusks to poke and scare each other.

This old bull has lost both his tusks. And another bull poked him beneath his right eye.

Walruses push and shove each other to get the best places to rest. They jab each other with their tusks. Sometimes they get hurt. But they usually aren't hurt badly because they have tough skin. Walrus skin is up to 1 inch thick.

Older bulls have lumps called tubercles (TOO-ber-kuhls) on their necks and shoulders. Tubercles make a bull's skin even thicker and tougher. Young bulls have smooth skin without any tubercles.

The lumpy bumps on this bull are called tubercles. Having tubercles is like wearing a coat of armor.

Each year, Pacific walruses travel up to 1,500 miles. But they don't swim the whole way. Sometimes they ride on floating pieces of ice called ice floes. In the spring, cows travel north. They stay north all summer long. Bulls travel south to the rocky islands off the coasts of Alaska and Russia.

These walruses are riding on an ice floe. The ride gives them a rest from swimming during long trips.

In the fall, the bulls want to be with the cows. So the bulls start moving north too. At the same time, the cows move south. Soon they meet the bulls. Then the cows and bulls stay together for the winter. In the spring, the cows move north once again. And the bulls move south.

Round Island, off the coast of Alaska, is a safe place for bulls to spend the summer.

Chapter 5

A walrus cow sits on an ice floe with her baby. When are baby walruses born?

Growing Up

 Walrus cows have babies in the spring. A young walrus is called a calf. A cow usually has one calf every two to three years.

Walrus cows teach their young how to hunt for food.

A calf can swim soon after it is born. But a calf has only a thin layer of blubber. The blubber is too thin to keep the calf warm. The mother helps keep the calf warm until its blubber gets thicker.

During its first weeks of life, a calf nurses often. When it nurses, it drinks its mother's milk. A walrus's milk has much more fat than a cow's milk. The fat helps the calf to grow quickly. Soon it has thick blubber. Then it can stay warm in the water.

The calf on the right is nursing.

Walrus calves grow quickly.

Walrus cows are good mothers. They touch their calves often. And they protect them from danger. A cow takes her calf with her when she goes hunting. That is how a calf learns to find food. A calf begins to eat solid food when it is

about six months old. But it still nurses too.
When the calf is two or three years old, it stops
nursing. Then it eats only solid food.

Walrus cows are taking good care of this calf.

Walrus calves learn how to swim soon after they are born.

When a calf is one year old, its tusks are about 1 inch long. But they are too short for anyone to see them from a distance. A calf's tusks can't be seen until it is about two years old.

Female calves become full-grown cows when they are 9 or 10 years old. Male calves become full-grown bulls when they are about 15 years old. Male calves may join a herd of bulls when they are just 4 or 5 years old. This is dangerous for a young bull. He may get crushed by a large bull. Or he may get hurt by a large bull's long tusks.

Young bulls, like the one in the center, sometimes get hurt by older bulls.

Chapter 6

Two walruses meet in the icy water near Alaska. How did the native people of North America use walruses?

People and Walruses

Native people in the far northern part of North America have hunted walruses for thousands of years. These people made boats from the walrus's thick skin. They made tools from its bones and tusks. They burned oil from walrus blubber for heat and light. And the meat from one walrus fed many people.

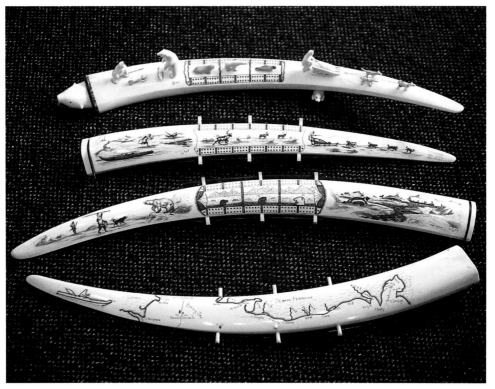

Whalers used to carve walrus tusks. Carved walrus tusks are called scrimshaw.

When the first white people came to the far north hundreds of years ago, there were about 300,000 walruses. More and more people arrived. Thousands of walruses were killed for oil and ivory. Finally there were only about 50,000 walruses left. But people made laws to protect walruses. Only a few walruses are killed anymore.

These Atlantic walruses are swimming in Hudson Bay, in Canada.

There are more walruses than there once were. Scientists believe that there are about 250,000 Pacific walruses. But Atlantic walruses are still rare. Only about 20,000 of them are still living.

Scientists learn about the lives of walruses by watching them. But it is hard for scientists to watch walruses during cold northern winters. And scientists can't see walruses who are swimming deep underwater. Much of the walrus's life is still a mystery.

Scientists count walruses when the animals are on land or ice. Scientists also study the way walruses live.

On Sharing a Book

As you know, adults greatly influence a child's attitude toward reading. When a child sees you read, or when you share a book with a child, you're sending a message that reading is important. Show the child that reading a book together is important to you. Find a comfortable, quiet place. Turn off the television and limit other distractions, such as telephone calls.

Be prepared to start slowly. Take turns reading parts of this book. Stop and talk about what you're reading. Talk about the photographs. You may find that much of the shared time is spent discussing just a few pages. This discussion time is valuable for both of you, so don't move through the book too quickly. If the child begins to lose interest, stop reading. Continue sharing the book at another time. When you do pick up the book again, be sure to revisit the parts you have already read. Most importantly, enjoy the book!

Be a Vocabulary Detective

You will find a word list on page 5. Words selected for this list are important to the understanding of the topic of this book. Encourage the child to be a word detective and search for the words as you read the book together. Talk about what the words mean and how they are used in the sentence. Do any of these words have more than one meaning? You will find these words defined in a glossary on page 46.

What about Questions?

Use questions to make sure the child understands the information in this book. Here are some suggestions:

> What did this paragraph tell us? What does this picture show? What do you think we'll learn about next? Could a walrus live in your backyard? Why/Why not? Where do walruses live? How do walruses protect themselves from the cold? What do walruses eat? How long does a young walrus stay with its mother? What do you think it's like to be a walrus? What is your favorite part of this book? Why?

If the child has questions, don't hesitate to respond with questions of your own such as: What do *you* think? Why? What is it that you don't know? If the child can't remember certain facts, turn to the index.

Introducing the Index

The index is an important learning tool. It helps readers get information quickly without searching throughout the whole book. Turn to the index on page 47. Choose an entry, such as *staying warm,* and ask the child to use the index to find out how a walrus's blubber helps it stay warm. Repeat this exercise with as many entries as you like. Ask the child to point out the differences between an index and a glossary. (The index helps readers find information quickly, while the glossary tells readers what words mean.)

Where in the World?

Many plants and animals found in the Early Bird Nature Books series live in parts of the world other than the United States. Encourage the child to find the places mentioned in this book on a world map or globe. Take time to talk about climate, terrain, and how you might live in such places.

All the World in Metric!

Although our monetary system is in metric units (based on multiples of 10), the United States is one of the few countries in the world that does not use the metric system of measurement. Here are some conversion activities you and the child can do using a calculator:

WHEN YOU KNOW:	MULTIPLY BY:	TO FIND:
miles	1.609	kilometers
feet	0.3048	meters
inches	2.54	centimeters
gallons	3.787	liters
tons	0.907	metric tons
pounds	0.454	kilograms

Activities

Make up a story about walruses. Be sure to include information from this book. Draw or paint pictures to illustrate your story.

Visit a zoo to see walruses. How are they similar to seals and sea lions? How are they different?

Pretend you are a walrus. How do you get food? How do you talk to other walruses? Where do you sleep? What happens when an enemy is near?

Glossary

blubber—a layer of fat that helps a walrus stay warm

bull—an adult male walrus

calf—a young walrus

cow—an adult female walrus

haul out—a place where walruses come on land

herds—groups of walruses

ice floes—floating pieces of ice

nurses—drinks its mother's milk

pinnipeds (PIN-nuh-pehdz)—ocean animals that have four flippers

predators (PREH-duh-turz)—animals who hunt and eat other animals

prey—animals who are hunted and eaten by other animals

throat sacs—sacs in walruses' throats that fill with air

tubercles (TOO-ber-kuhls)—lumps on the skin of older male walruses

tusks—long teeth that stick out of a walrus's mouth

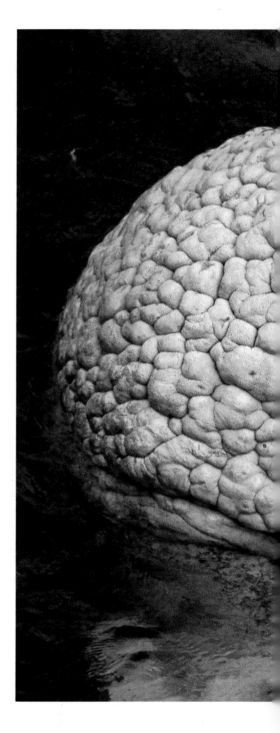

Index

Pages listed in **bold** type refer to photographs.

babies, 33–39

color, 15, **17**

eating, 19–20, 35, 36–37

flippers, 7, **9**, 10–11

hunting, 18–19

kinds of walruses, 12–13

people and walruses, 40–43

size, 6
skin, 29, 30
sleeping, 20–21
sounds, 23–24
staying warm, 13–14, 34, 35
swimming, **9**, 10–11, 16, 20–**22**, 34

teeth, 7–9, **10**, **12**, 27–29, 38

whiskers, 19, **20**

The Early Bird Nature Books Series

African Elephants	Horses	Sandhill Cranes
Alligators	Jellyfish	Scorpions
Ants	Manatees	Sea Lions
Apple Trees	Moose	Sea Turtles
Bobcats	Mountain Goats	Slugs
Brown Bears	Mountain Gorillas	Swans
Cats	Peacocks	Tarantulas
Cockroaches	Penguins	Tigers
Cougars	Polar Bears	Venus Flytraps
Crayfish	Popcorn Plants	Vultures
Dandelions	Prairie Dogs	Walruses
Dolphins	Rats	Whales
Giant Sequoia Trees	Red-Eyed Tree Frogs	White-Tailed Deer
Herons	Saguaro Cactus	Wild Turkeys